BAD SCIENCE JOKES

Published: Self. February 2016

Along with BadScienceJokes online.

Jokes assembled by Melissa Miller.

Cover design by Melissa Miller using the tools of PixlrExpress.

BadScienceJokes online sites owned and operated solely by Melissa Miller.

BadScienceJokes, Melissa Miller, or the accounts and platforms BadScienceJokes uses are not in cooperation with this book or BadScienceJokes in any way.

Bad Science Jokes is a self published book in cooperation with the BadScienceJokes blog on assorted social media sites. This book is in no way associated with any website. This is a collection of jokes off the BadScienceJokes blog online made into print. Jokes are in no way copyrighted and cannot be saved. Not all were originally written by the blog owner of BadScienceJokes and BadScienceJokes does not take ownership of any of the jokes in this work.

This book is dedicated to everyone who ever had to listen to me tell a joke. I'm sorry. This doesn't make up for it in the least bit.

Also, my parents and sister who indirectly (or directly) helped me with this and the blog. And my group in high school science class, junior year. I haven't heard from you all in years but-thanks.

Table Of Contents

Pages 4 -54 : Middle School

Pages 54- 113 : High School

Pages 114 - 155: Scientist

Middle School

These jokes will be science, math and other educational jokes for all those with a basic science understanding!

Get ready to laugh!

What's up?

Space.

Two scientists got in a fight.

"Let me atom" they yelled!

Where does bad light end up?

In a prism!

Why don't you take these

bad science jokes

and barium?!

I hired a man to do 8
odd-jobs for me.
When I got back, he'd
only done jobs
1, 3, 5, and 7.

You know what really brings me down?

Gravity.

I tell chemistry jokes periodically.

Oxygen and Magnesium went on a date.

OMg!

Which element is related to you?

BROmine

Isn't gold Ausome?

Why did the math teacher keep a ruler under his pillow?

To see how long he could sleep.

Biology grows on you.

Anything that doesn't matter,
has no mass.

Scientists studying the
sun have a
flare for research.

Math teachers have a lot of problems.

How did the geology student drown?

His grades were below C-level.

I stayed up all night to see where the sun went and then it dawned on me.

What did the chemist take when he was told his breath stinks?

Ele-mints.

Why are chemists never able to prank their friends?

They lack the element of surprise.

Did you hear about the kidnapping at the school?

He woke up.

You know what's odd?

Numbers not divisible by two.

Math teachers call retirement "the aftermath"

Astronomy is looking up!

I wanted to make a joke about iron but didn't want to pay the fe.

Science Teacher: Oxygen is a must for breathing & for life. It was discovered in 1773.

Student: Thank God I was born after 1773. Otherwise I would have died without it.

I learned about the colon through the process of elimination.

Thanks for explaining the word "many" to me,

it means a lot.

A volcano is a mountain
with hiccups

I paid $20 for a college education.
I brought my ladder to class and got a higher education.

Skipping school to bungee jump will get you suspended.

A theory on geology was recently developed. Some opposing scientists tried to disprove it, but the facts were rock solid.

You want to hear some facts about clouds?

Never mind, they're over your head...

You can't run through a
campground.
You can only ran.
Since its past tents.

Why did the weatherman bring a bar of soap to work?

He was predicting showers

Why do museums have so many old dinosaur bones?

Because they can't find any new ones.

A school kid asks his teacher "Is it true that the law of gravity keeps us on Earth?"

The teacher replied, "Yes."

The kid then asked, "What kept us down before the law was passed?"

What's a math teacher's favorite type of toilet paper?

Multiply

Which eukaryotic organism throws the best parties?

The Fungi!

The
optical scientist who
stole his colleague's
bifocals was sentenced
to three years in a state
prism.

Isaac Newton?
More like Isaac Knew
TONS

I learned how to greet
people in
Hi School.

Throws calculator at you

You weren't counting on that were you?

I wondered why my geometry class was always tired.

They were all out of shape.

Every day is pi day if you're a mathematician or a chef.

What US state has the most math teachers?

Mathachussets

Noses are in the middle of your face because they enjoy being the scent-er of attention.

What's a scientist's favorite flavor of gum?

Ex-spearmint

Why did the germ cross the microscope?

To get to the other slide

If you're studying Niels Bohr, are you Borh-ing?

How much room is needed for fungi to grow?

As mushroom as possible

High School

The following jokes are aimed at those with a high school level education.

Otherwise known as, someone who understands a bit more about science principles and phrases than the average person.

Do you understand them all?

My teacher threw
sodium chloride at me,
that's a salt.

I'm as anti-social as a noble gas.

A roman walks into a bar,
holds up two fingers and says,

"5 beers please".

Flowers are not fond of gun control.
They want to hang on to their *pistil*.

Who is the hottest scientist?

Robert Boyle

Graphing is where I draw the line!

Math puns are the first sine of madness!

Someone called me
average.
How mean!

Do you have 11 protons? Because you are sodium fine.

I'm centripetal force because I don't do any work.

Protons have mass?
I didn't know they were Catholic!

What do you zinc about elemental puns?

The rotation of the earth
makes my day!

The first scientists who
studied fog
were *mistified*.

What was the geometry student looking for at the beach?

A tangent.

These physics jokes are so bad it hertz!

I put root beer in a square cup and now it's just beer.

Actually, alcohol is a solution.

Having to do trigonometry should be considered a sin!

I think I lost an electron,

I better keep an ion that.

There's a fine line between a numerator and denominator.

Einstein developed a theory about space and you know, it was about time too!

Arteries hold a special place in my heart.

My physics teacher said I had potential then threw me off the roof.

What do plants do when other plants are sad?

Photo-sympathize

There are 10 types of people in the world, those who understand binary and those who don't.

Color is a pigment of your imagination.

Why didn't the gold atom date any francium atoms?

The gold atom was looking for a more stable relationship.

The first order of priority in hiring math majors is get them to sine on the dotted line

I realized I was getting old when a geologist dated me...

If a lightning bolt hits the back of a train, how long will it take to reach the driver?

Well, It depends if he's a good conductor.

Where do meteorologists go after work?

The isobar

Deaf mathematicians communicate through sine language.

I have a new theory on inertia but it doesn't seem to be gaining momentum

"I've got a big apatite", said the geologist

All you have to do in chem is try.

Do you already know the latest stats joke?

Probably

I tell chemistry jokes periodically.

Telling your geography teacher to get lost isn't the insult you were going for.

How do you make soup golden?

Add 24 carrots.

A chef transferred into
my chemistry class,
He almost licked the
spoon.

I've never been a good swimmer, my DNA almost drowned in its gene pool.

What did one lab rat say to the other?

"I've got my scientist so well trained that every time I push that buzzer, he brings me a snack!"

A sign hanging on a laboratory door: "Gone Nuclear Fission."

What do you call a microbiologist in an orchestra?

A cell-ist.

Why is electricity so dangerous?

Because it doesn't know how to conduct itself properly.

Don't bother me when
I'm doing chemistry.
I'm in my element.

What do you call an acid with an attitude?

A-mean-oh acid.

Old mathematicians never die;
they just lose some of their functions

After I left geometry class my life felt pointless.

What did the brain say to the nociceptor?

"You're a real pain, you know that?"

The geologists were depressed because they were being taken for granite.

I was gonna make a joke about sodium and hydrogen… but NaH.

Why didn't the two 4s eat dinner?

They already 8.

The concept of soap is pretty basic.

Teachers who take class attendance are absent-minded.

One day on Mercury lasts approximately 1408 hours.
The same as one Monday on Earth.

What does a mathematician call the occupied restroom on an airplane?

Hy-pot-en-use

Scientists

The following jokes are a bit tricky if you are not familiar with scientific theories or names. Some of these jokes will have you searching the internet for an explanation. There is also one joke in this list that is a bit inappropriate although you wouldn't know that unless you know what it means. Just a warning for parents-but don't worry!

I slapped my neon all these science jokes.

Why did the chicken cross the mobius strip?

To get to the same side

How many theoretical physicists specializing in general relativity does it take to change a light bulb?

Two. One to hold the bulb and one to rotate the universe.

There is a sign in Munich that says, "Heisenberg might have slept here."

"Knock knock."

Who's there?
"Interrupting coefficient of friction."

Interrupting coeffici-

"μ!!!!!"

A chemist, a physicist, and a biologist go to the beach. The physicist is intrigued by the waves, walks into the ocean to examine them and drowns.
The biologist is intrigued by the various forms of life, walks into the ocean to study them, and drowns.
The chemist is sitting on the beach with a lab notebook and writes
"Biologists and physicists are soluble in water.

x^2 and e^x are at a party.
x^2 is having a blast, but e^x is sitting in a corner by himself.
Eventually, x^2 comes over and says, "Hey e^x, why don't you try a bit harder to integrate?"
e^x replies, "It's no use. It wouldn't make a difference."

What is the difference between an entomologist and an etymologist?

An etymologist knows.

How does a mathematician determine the shortest fence to include a herd of cattle?

He draws a fence around his feet and declares *"I'm outside the fence"*.

An electron is driving down a motorway, and a policeman pulls him over. The policeman says:
"Sir, do you realize you were travelling at 130km per hour?"
The electron goes: "Oh great, now I'm lost."

A woman comes home to find her string theorist husband in bed with another woman. "But honey," he says, "I can explain everything!"

Two retired professors were vacationing with their wives at a hotel in the Bahamas. They were sitting on the porch one summer evening, watching the sun set.

The history professor asked the psychology professor, "Have you read Marx?"

To which the professor of psychology replied, "Yes and I think it's these pesky wicker chairs."

Most people believe that if it ain't broke, don't fix it.
Engineers believe that if it ain't broke, it doesn't have enough features yet.

Why does it never rain inside a barn?

Because it's a stable atmosphere.

Schrodinger's cat walks
into a bar.
And doesn't.

What do you get when you cross a joke with a rhetorical question?

Why are quantum physicists bad in bed?

Because when they have the momentum, they can't find the position

How can you tell the difference between a chemist and a plumber?

Ask them to pronounce "unionized."

Why didn't Sine cross the road?

Cosecant.

Calculus and alcohol don't mix.

Don't drink and derive.

Why were the Romans so bad at algebra?

They always ended up with X equals 10.

Three engineering students were gathered together discussing who must have designed the human body.
One said, "It was a mechanical engineer. Just look at all the joints."
"Another said, "No, it was an electrical engineer. The nervous system has many thousands of electrical connections."
The last one said, "No, actually it had to have been a civil engineer. Who else would run a toxic waste pipeline through a recreational area?"

When I saw a depressed mathematician I asked, *"What sum adder with you?"*

Why did the chicken cross the road?

The intermediate value theorem.

What did the femur say to the patella?

I kneed you.

What's the difference between a dog and a marine biologist?

One wags a tail and the other tags a whale.

Comathematicians are machines for turning cotheorems into ffee.

Are you a quantum tunneling particle?

Because your penetration depth is impressive.

Why did the chemist's pants keep falling down?

He had no *acetol*.

You know what's cool?

Things with low molecular motion.

A student is lucky enough to be riding on a train with Einstein and excitedly asks him, "Professor, does Boston stop at this train?"

There is no reason to judge protons and neutrons. They all have quarks.

The power went out in a jail cell so they called the mitochondria.

I feel bad for elements,
They only have the periodic table.

What do elements eat off of when it isn't there?

How to make a mathematician uncomfortable?

Put an exclamation mark after all of your answers

Why didn't Newton invent group theory?

Because he wasn't Abel.

Organic chemistry is difficult.

Students have alkynes of trouble.

Pavlov? Hmm, that rings a bell.

Resistance begins at ohm.

Werner Heisenberg, Kurt Gödel, and Noam Chomsky walk into a bar. Heisenberg turns to the other two and says, "Clearly this is a joke, but how can we figure out if it's funny or not?" Gödel replies, "We can't know that because we're inside the joke." Chomsky says, "Of course it's funny. You're just telling it wrong."

What do you call a baby sheep stuck in a fast-flowing river?

Laminar flow

A chemist, a biologist and a statistician are out hunting.
The chemist shoots at a deer missing 5 feet to the right.
The biologist then takes a shot and misses 5 feet to the left.
The statistician yells "We got 'em!"

Thanks for reading!

Melissa Miller loves working on BadScienceJokes and talking to people in all fields of science! Who knows, will there be a volume two? Keep updated with us by searching "badsciencejokes" on the internet! She would love to hear how you liked the book!

CPSIA information can be obtained
at www.ICGtesting.com
Printed in the USA
LVHW100946061221
705403LV00011B/235